Coloring for Animal Lovers
Lunawind Design
Illustrations by Crysten Nesseth
Layout by Elise Matheny

Inspired by our animal friends and the wild creatures we admire. Together we can protect the future of our planet. Color with the Lunawind Design Community.

Follow us on Facebook and post your coloring creations for everyone to admire!

Join us on Instagram @lunawinddesign
Visit us online for special web exclusives
www.lunawind.com

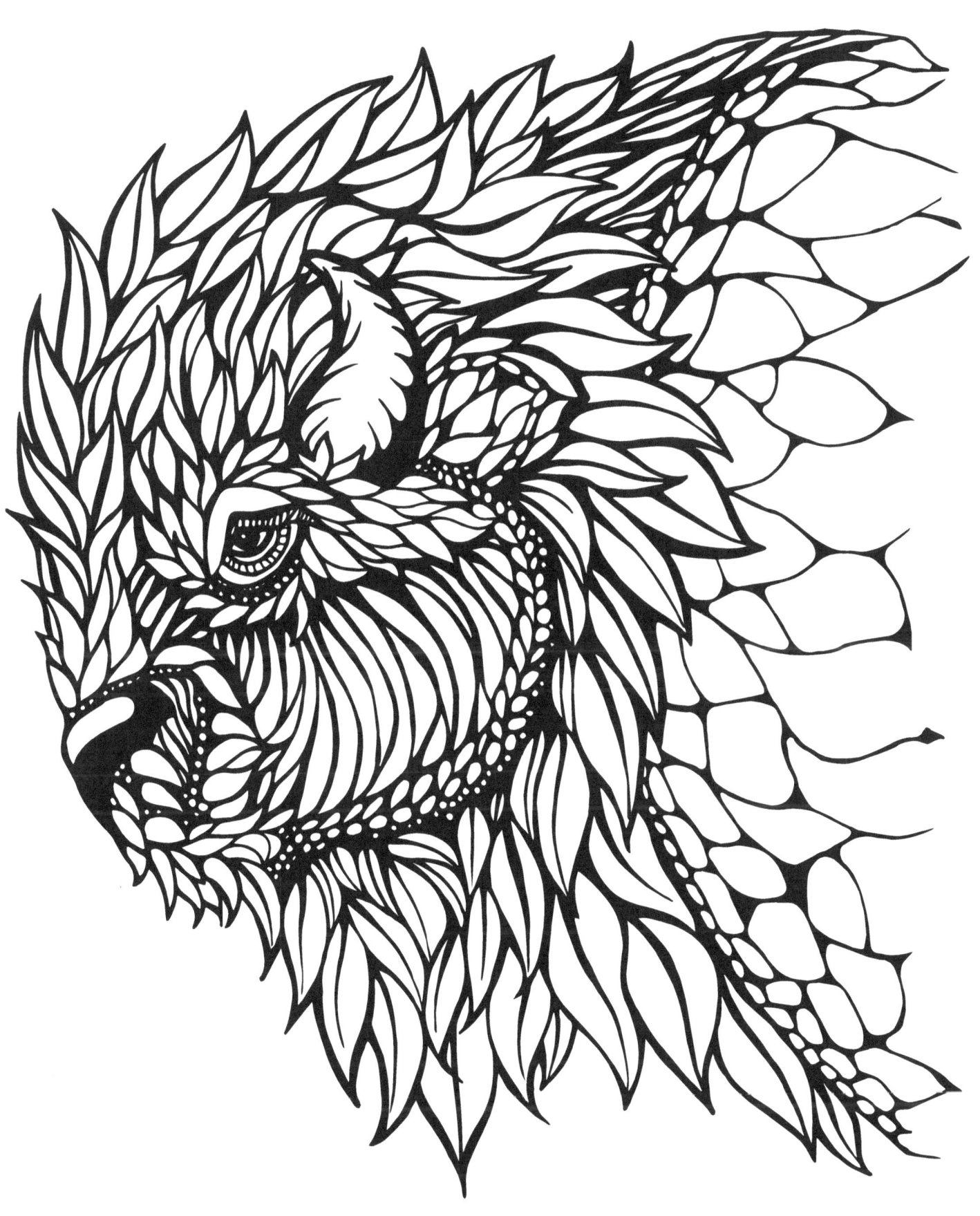

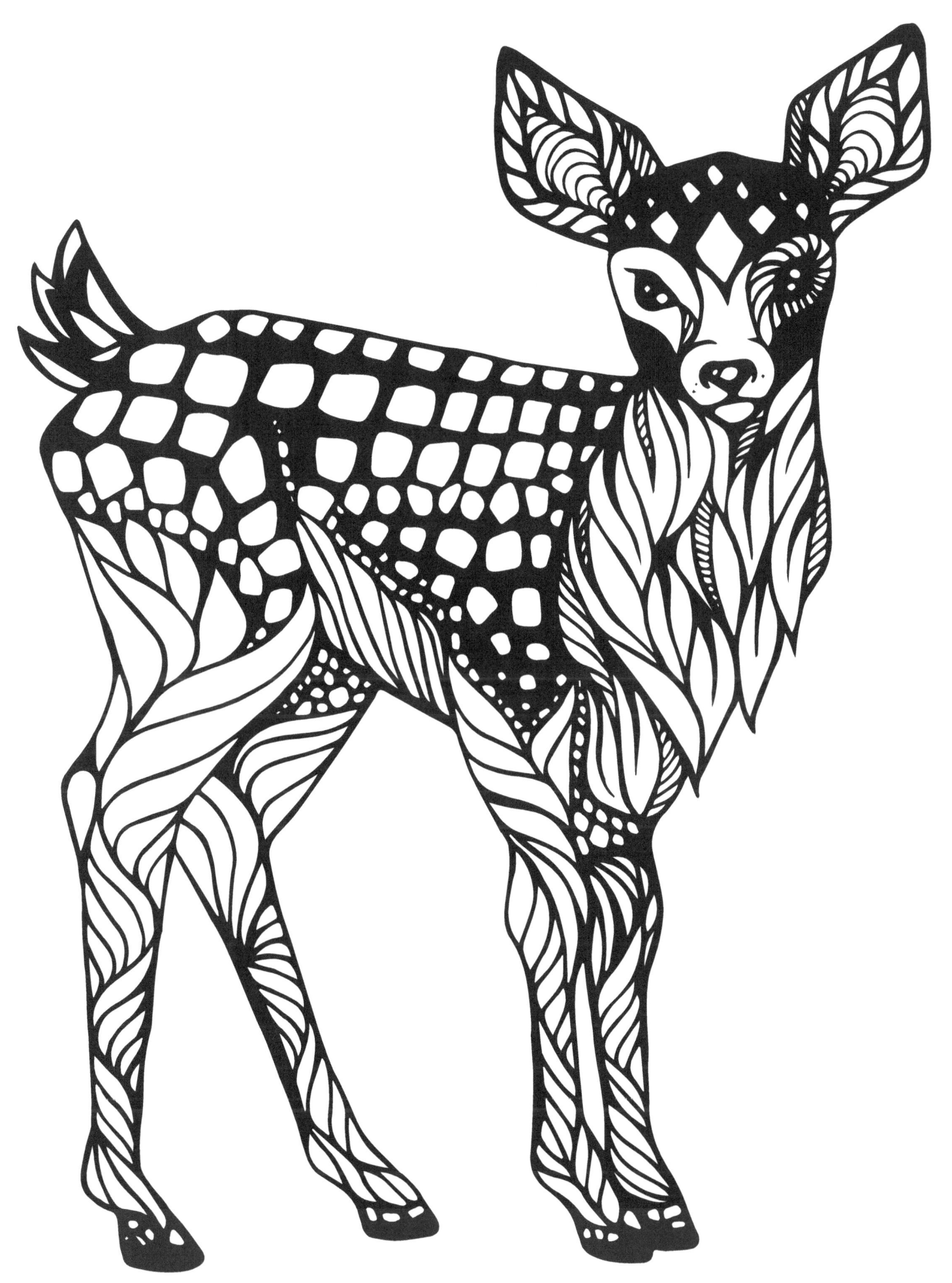

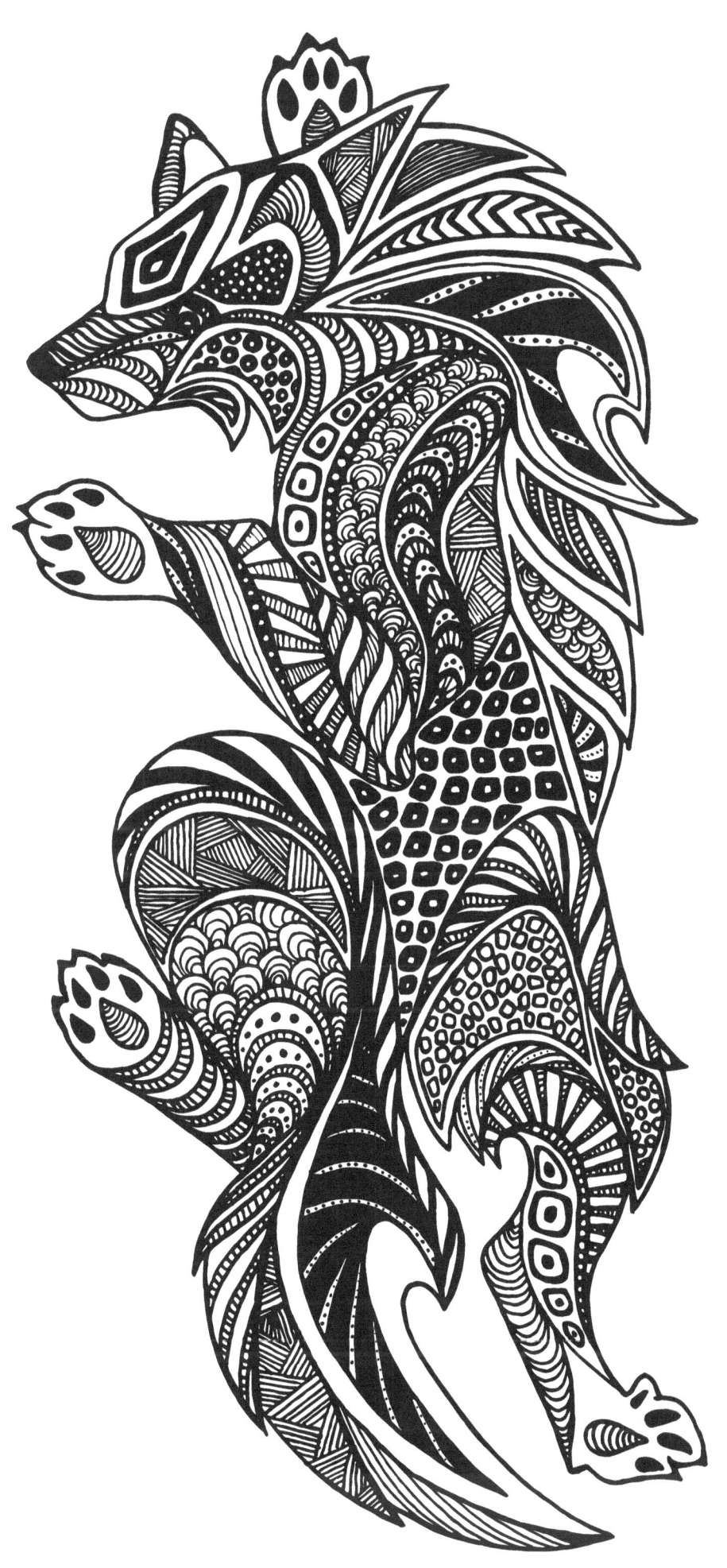

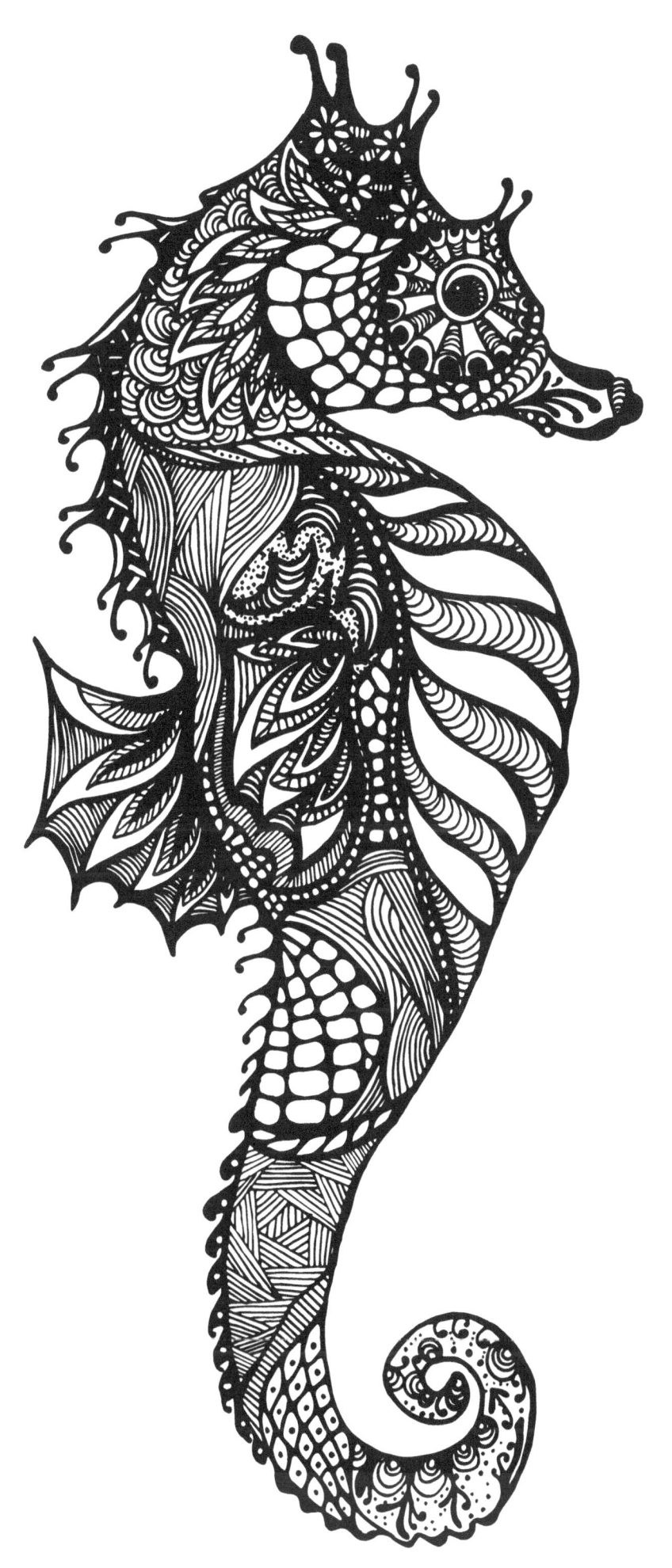

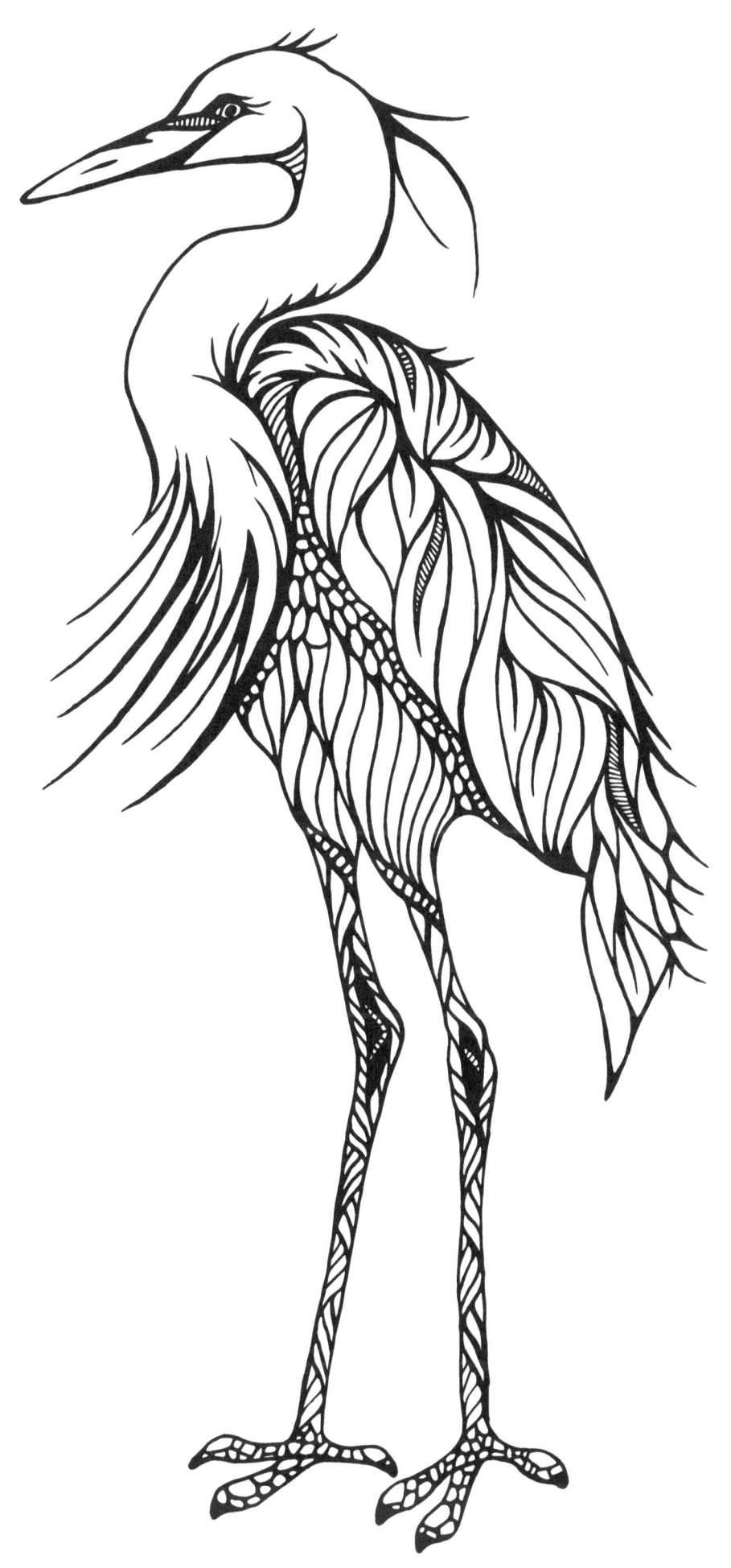

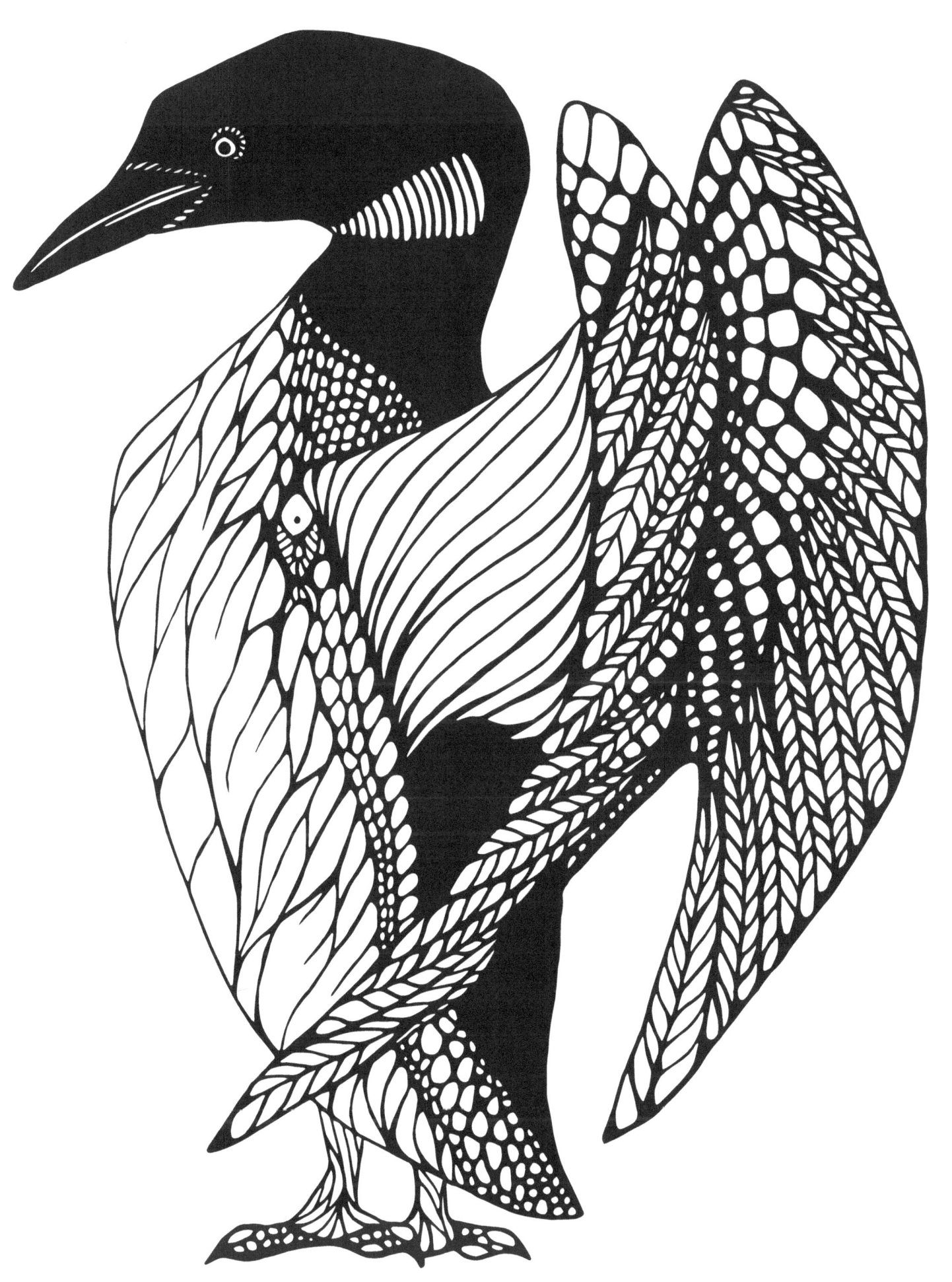

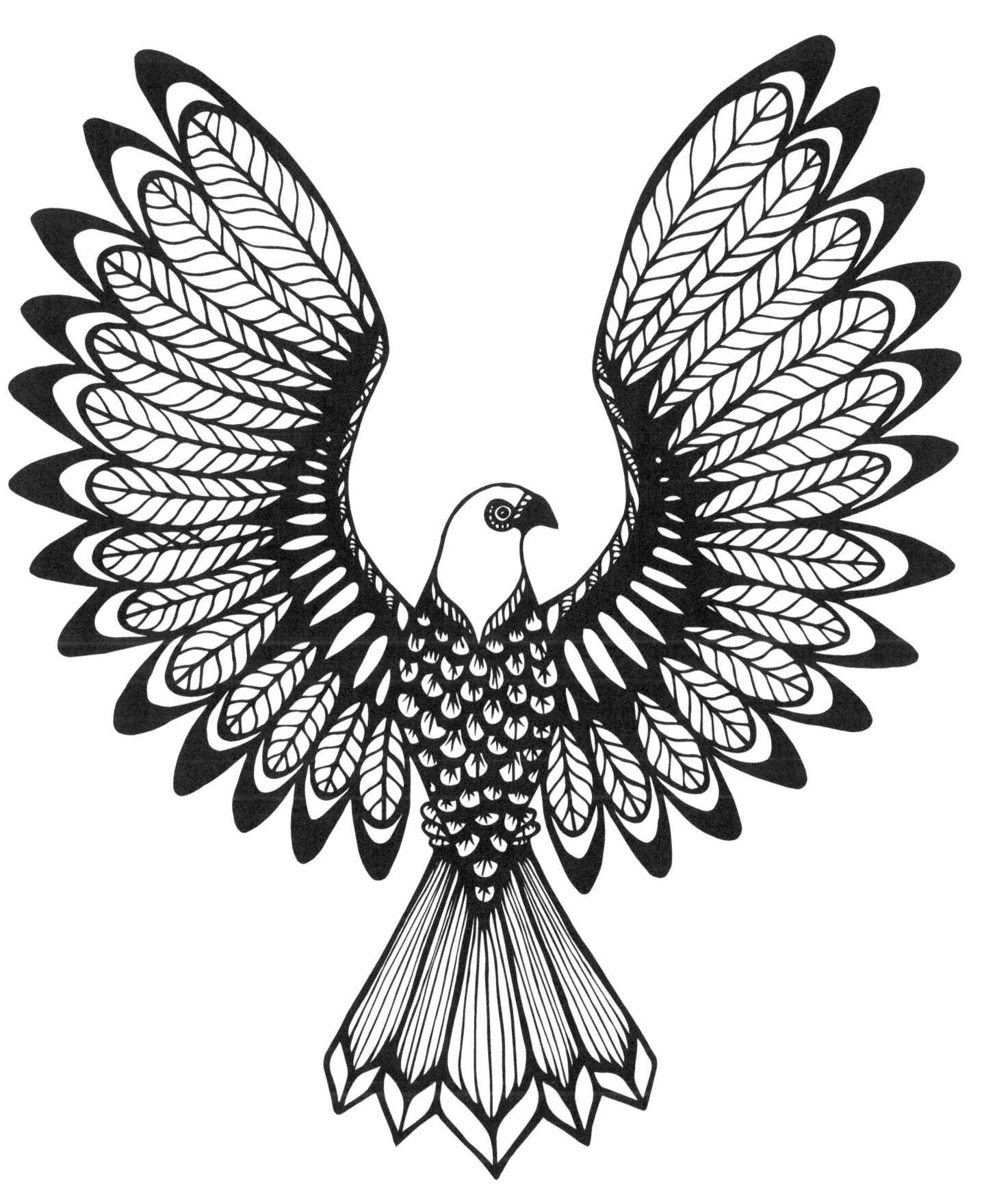

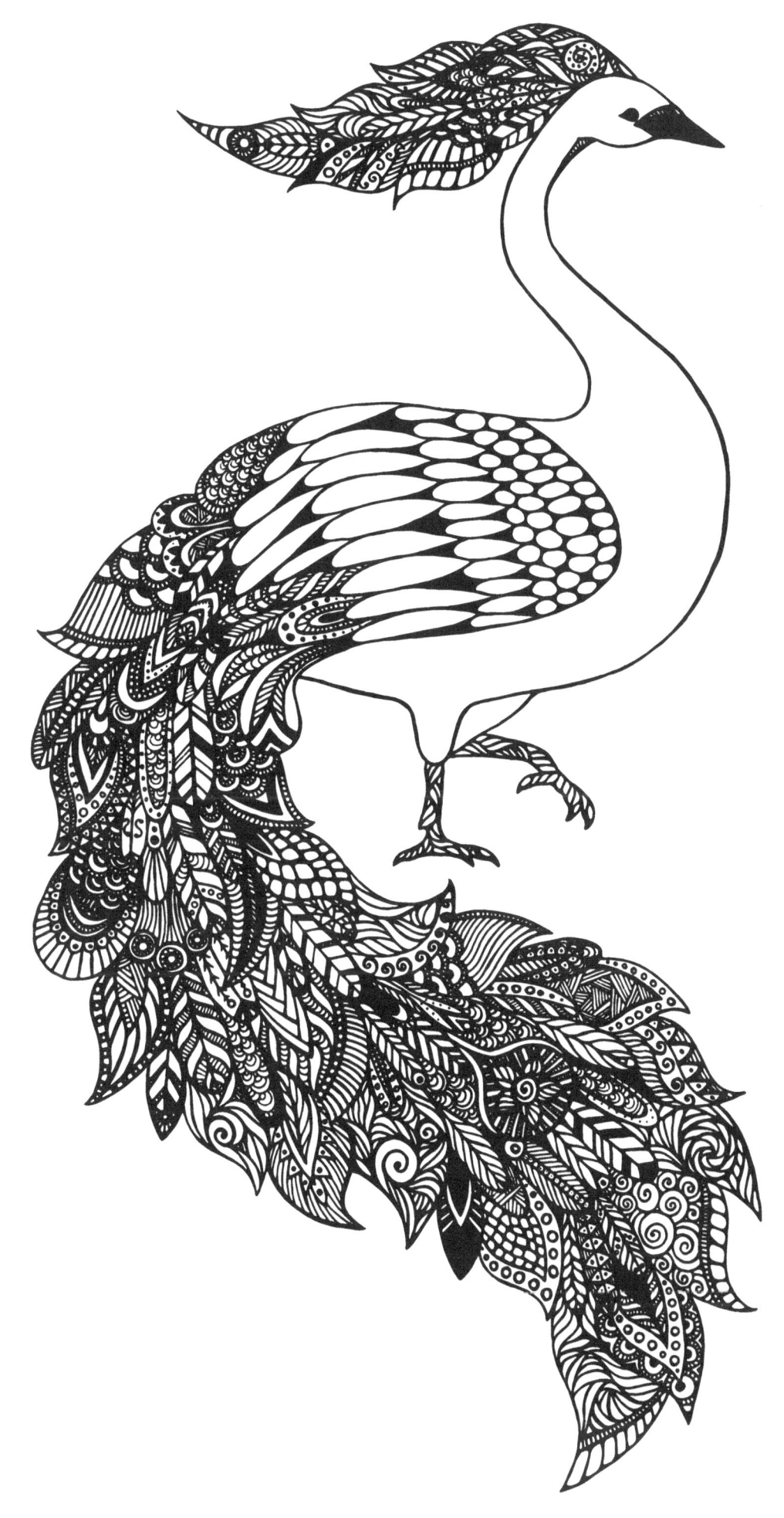

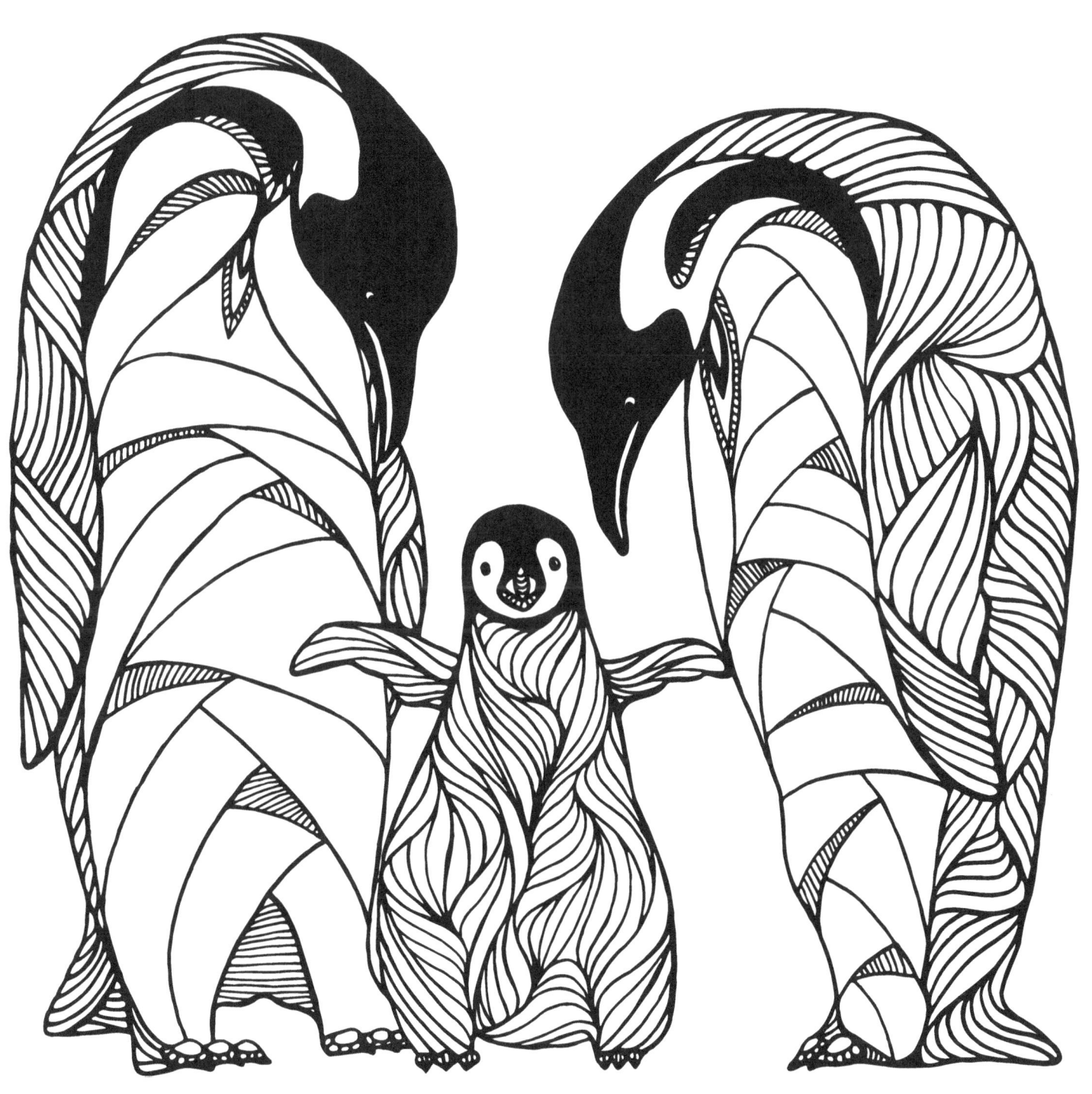

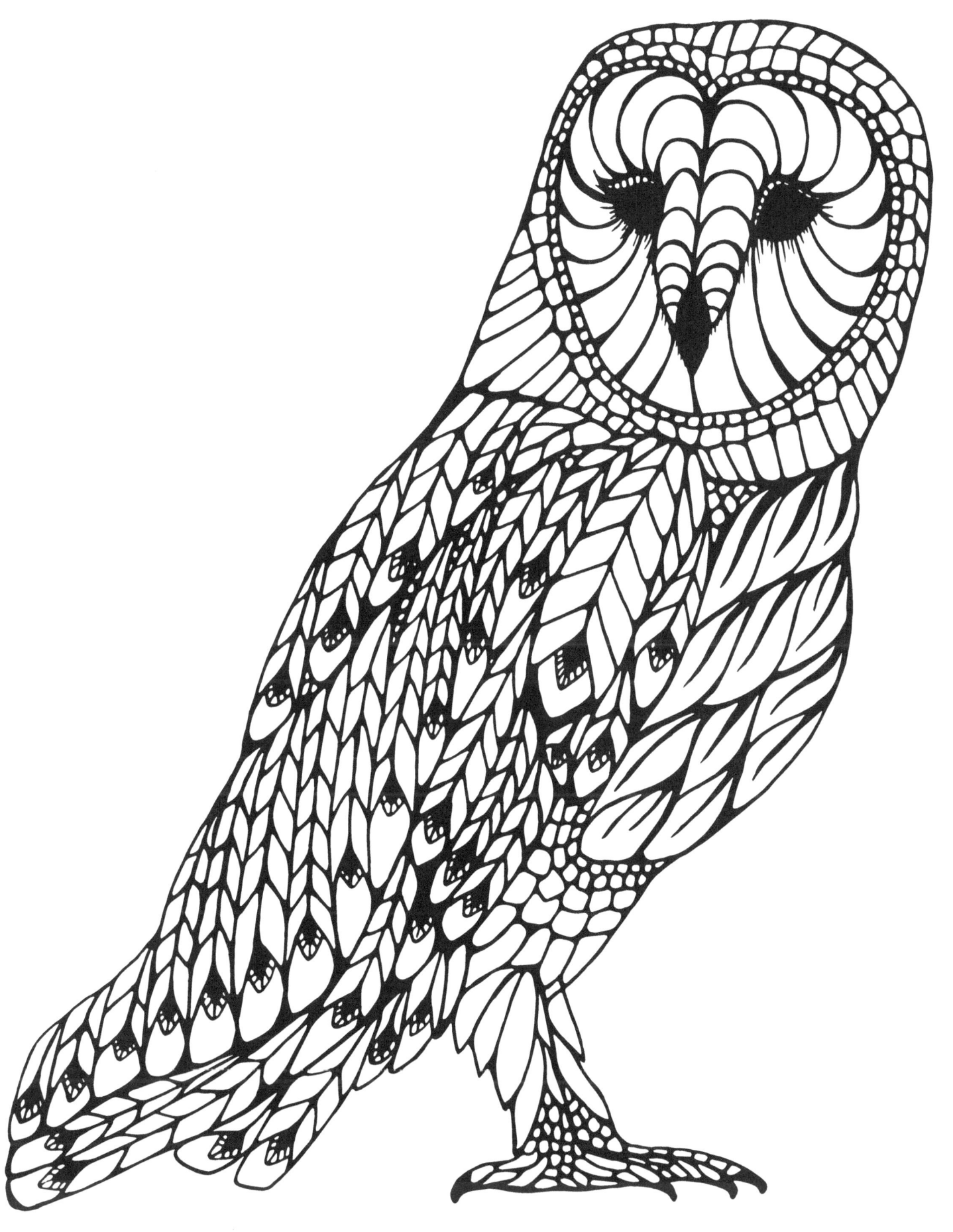

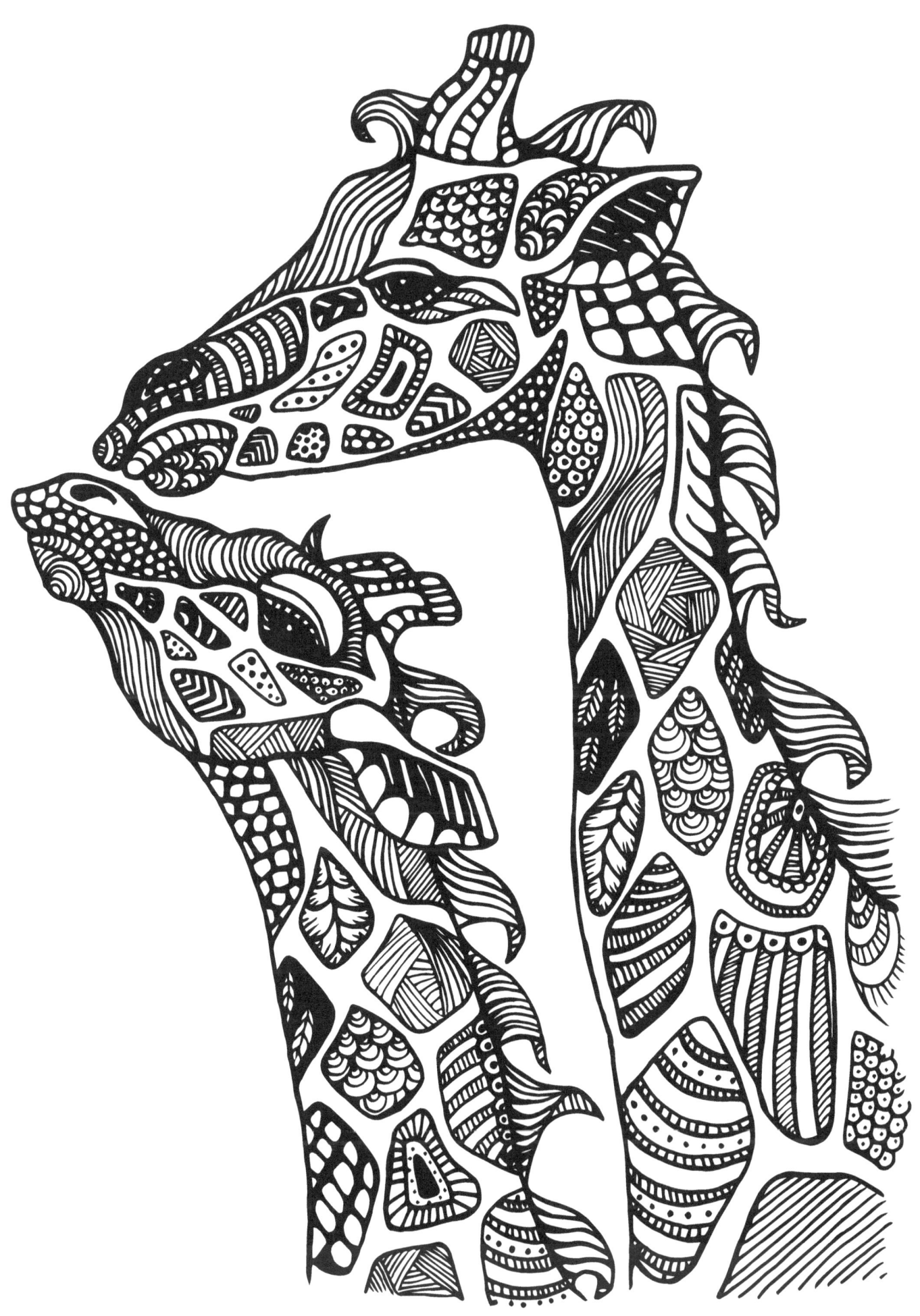

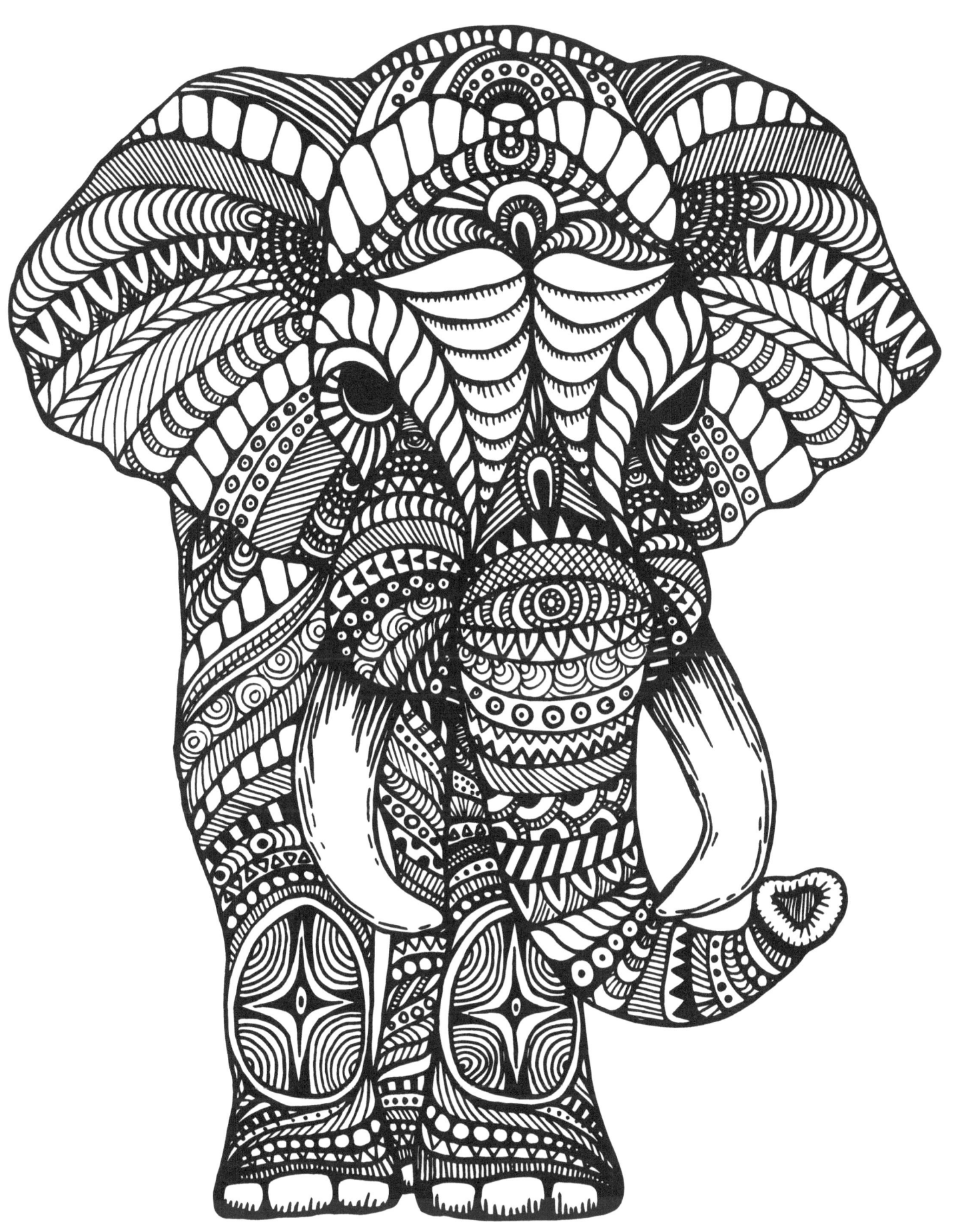

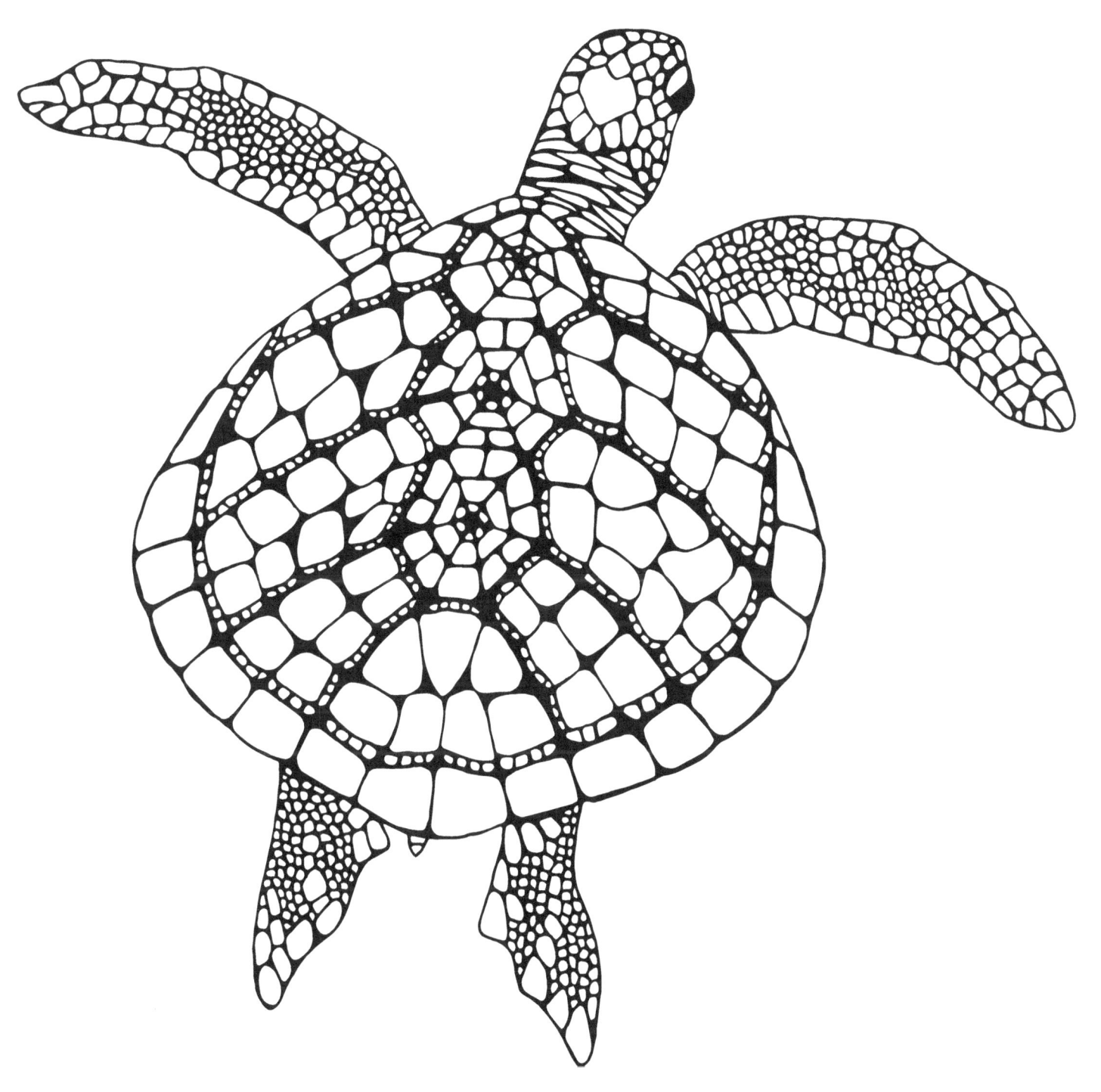

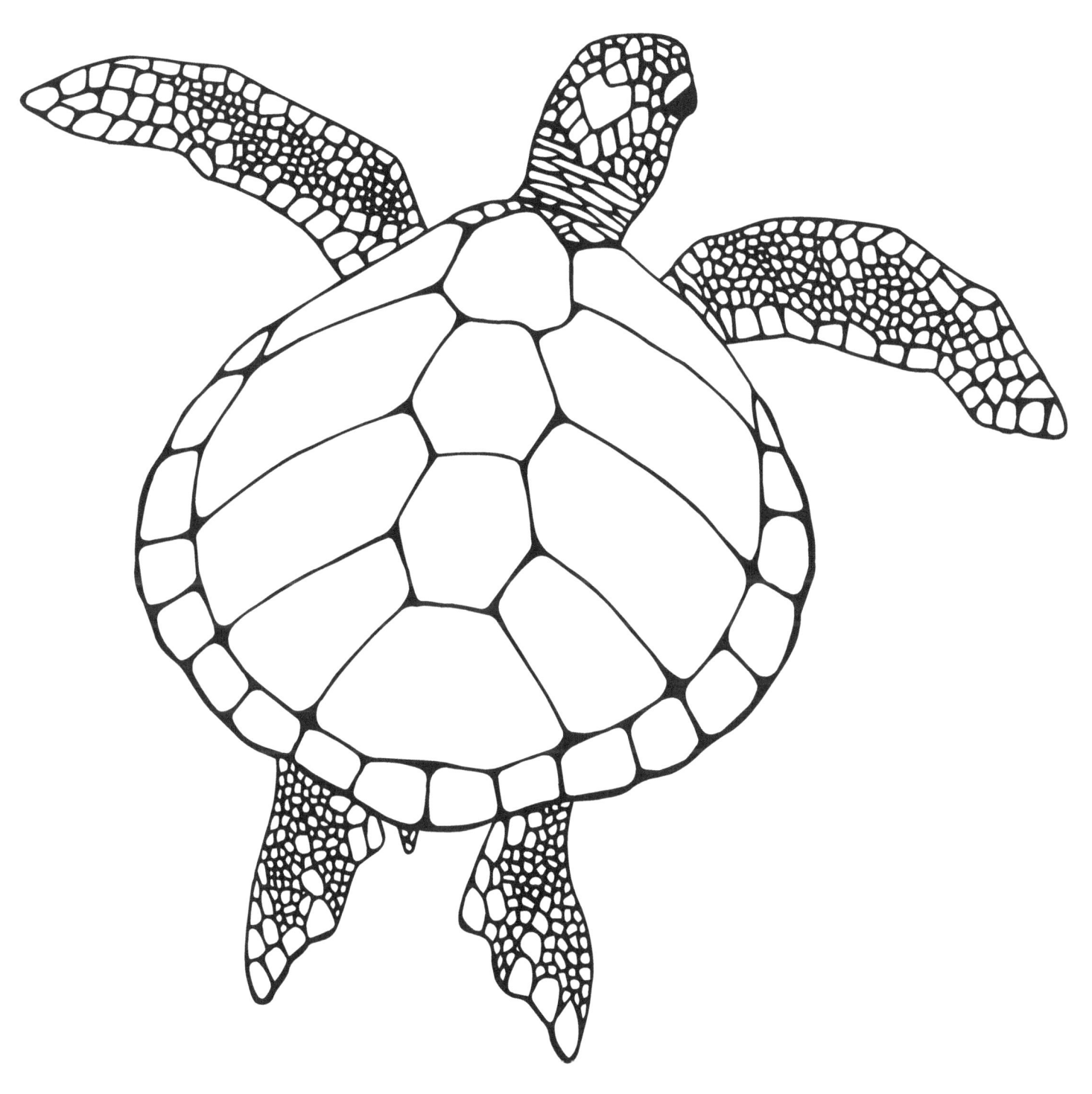

Feeling inspired? Try drawing your own shell pattern.

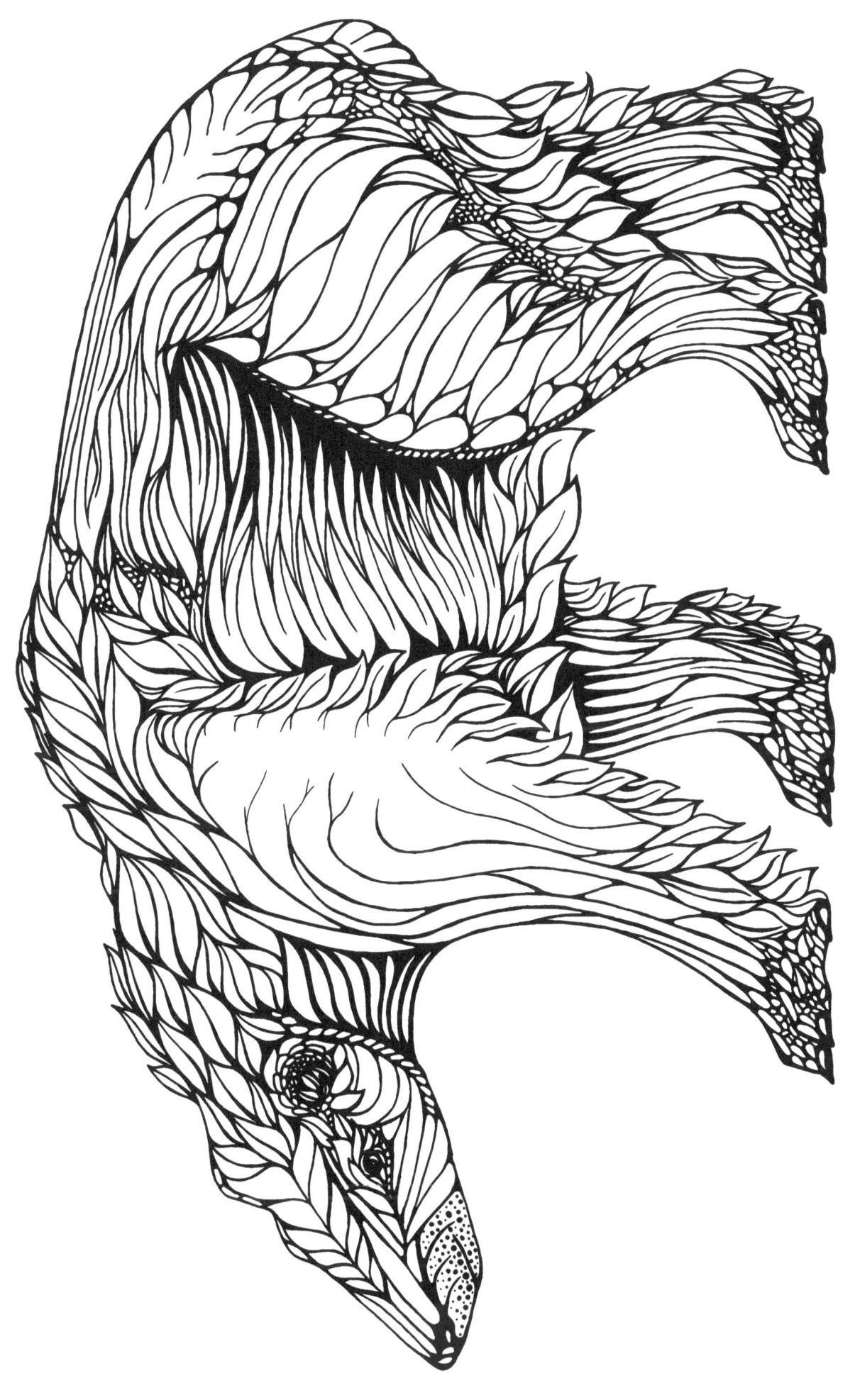

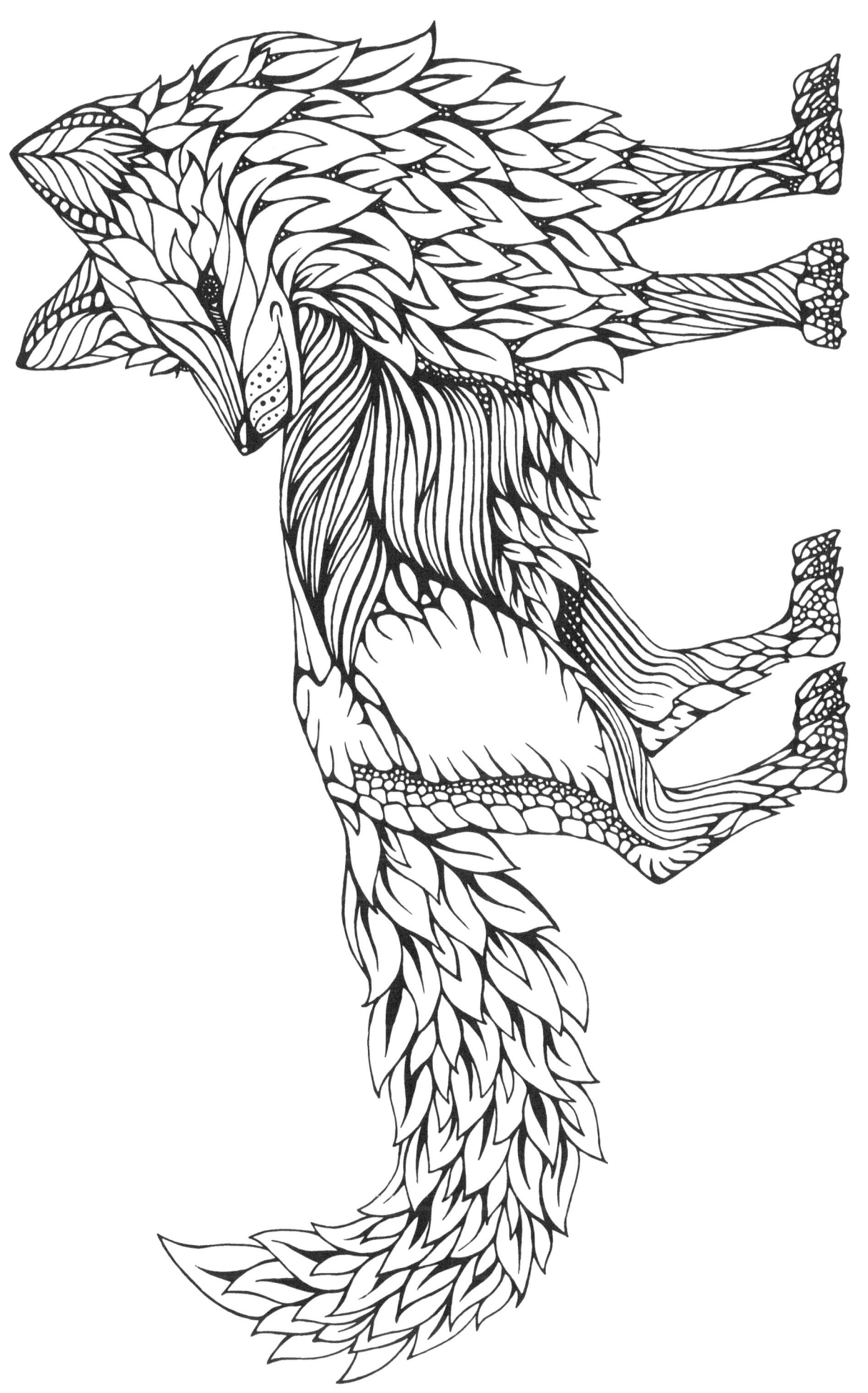

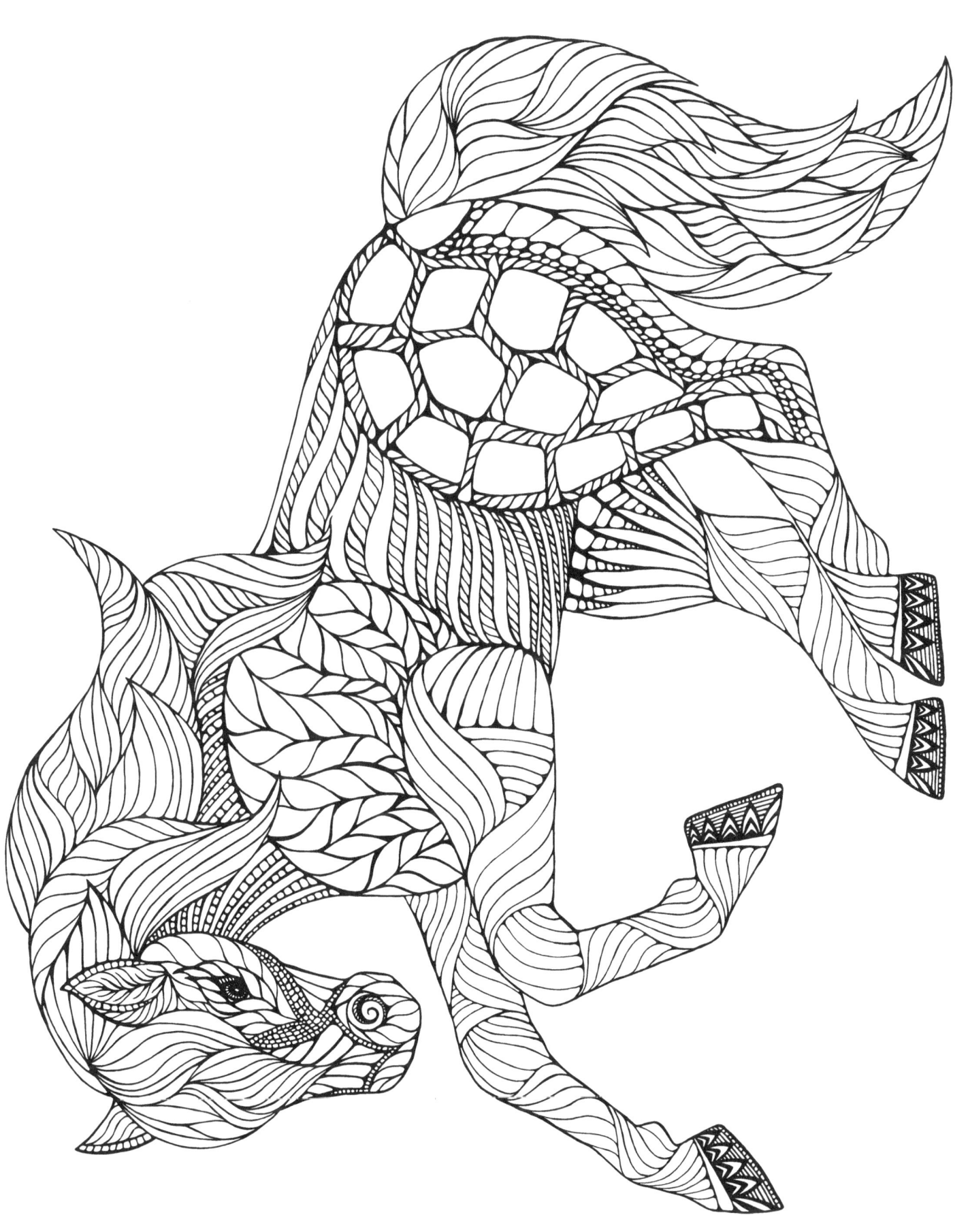

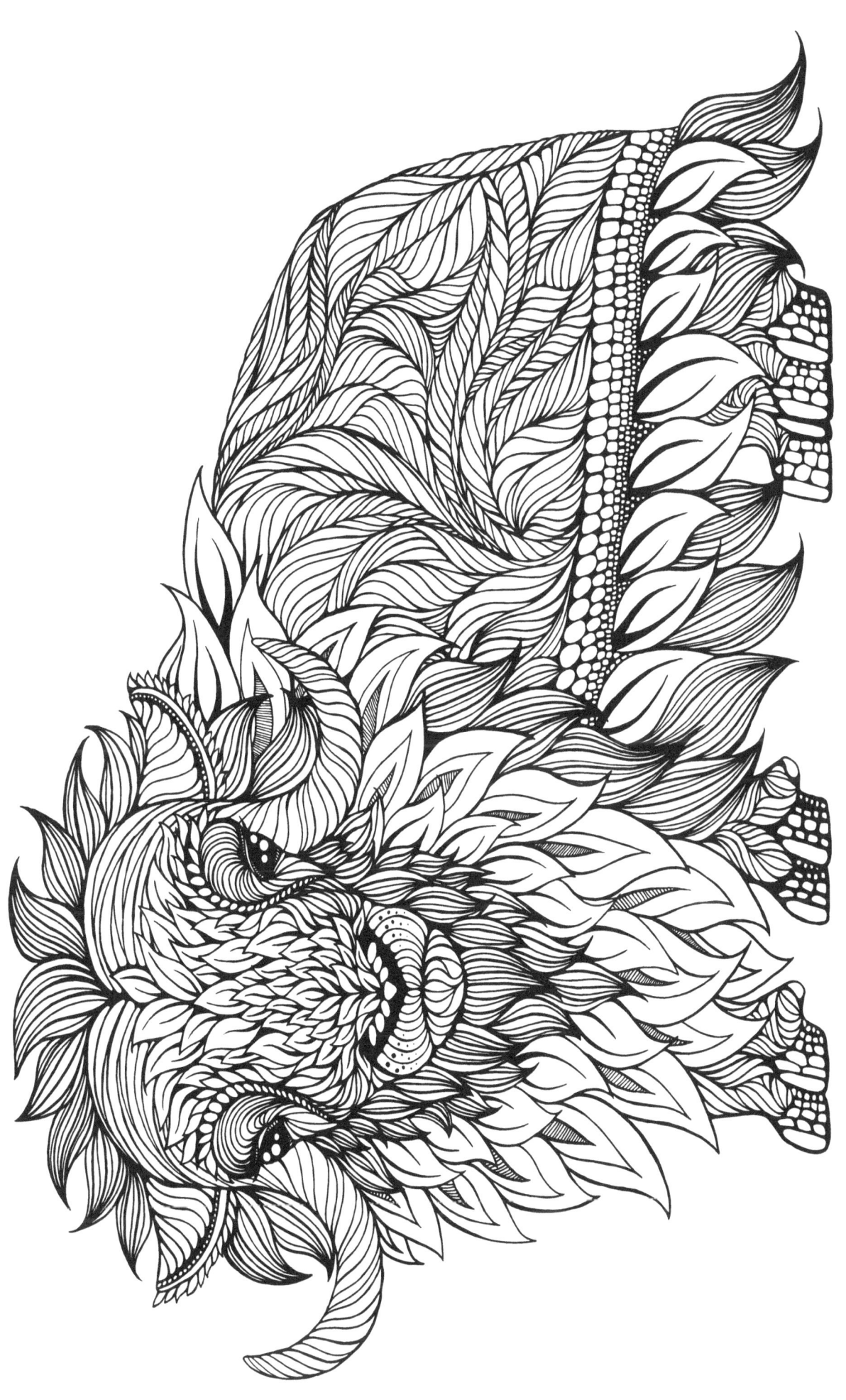

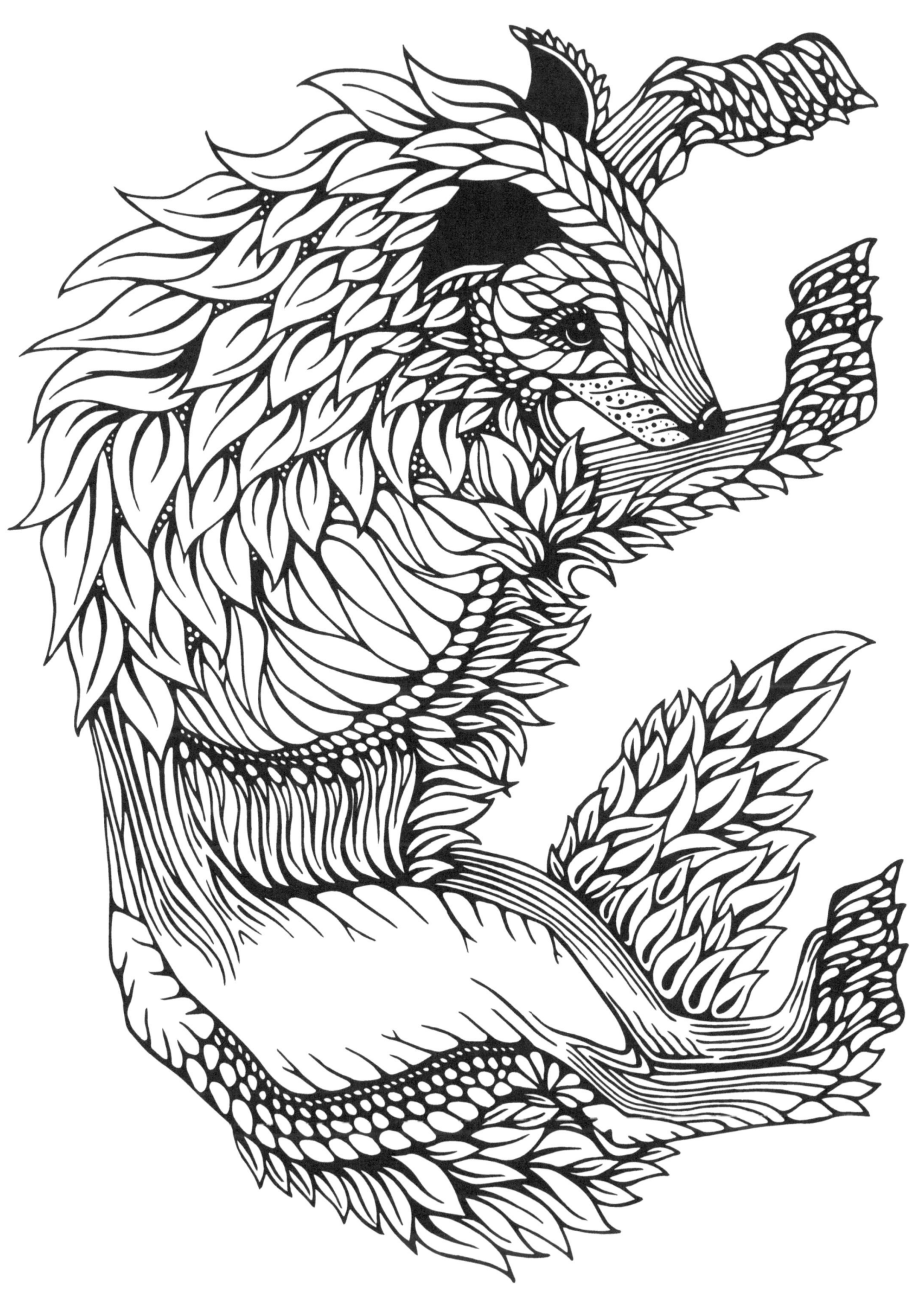

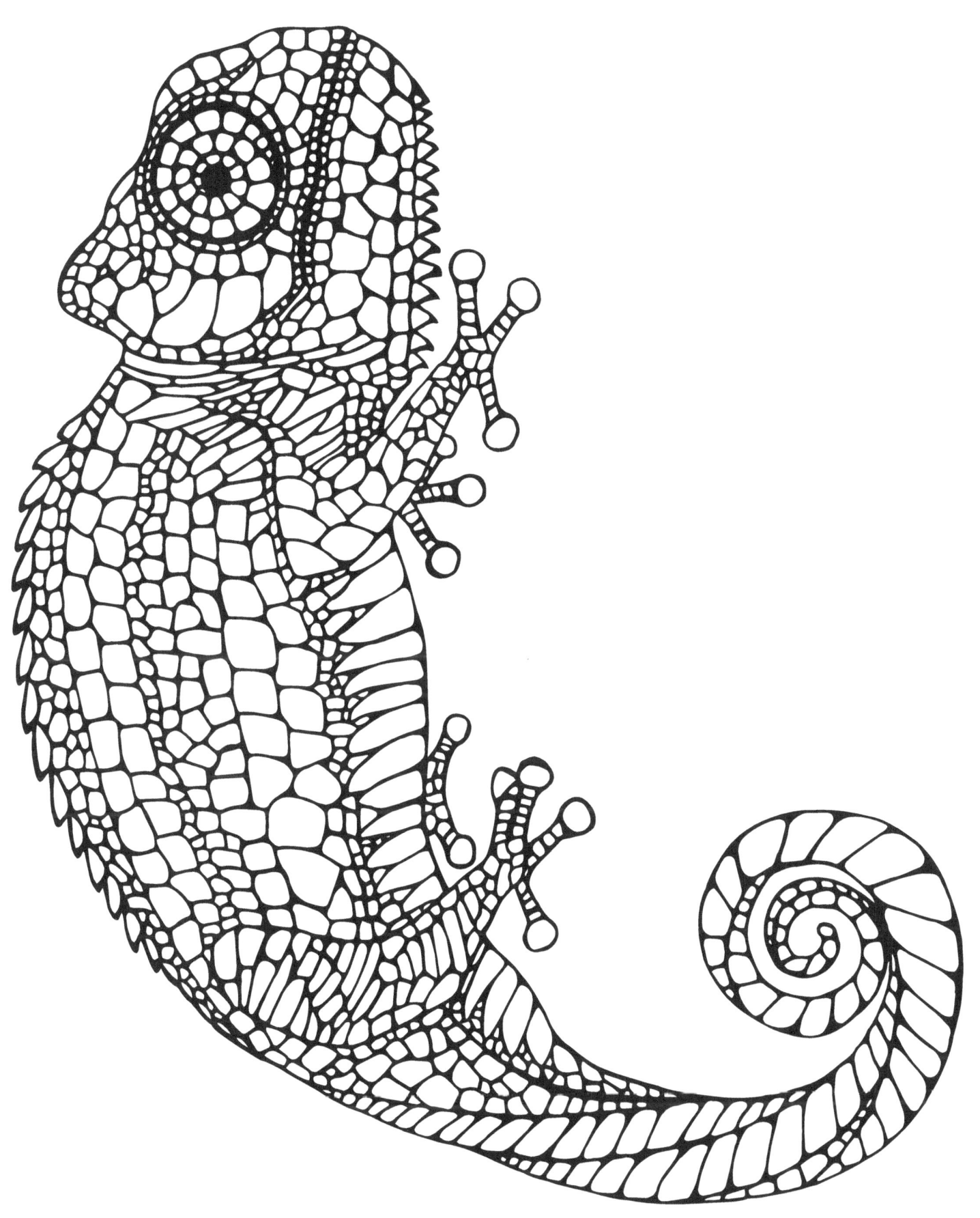

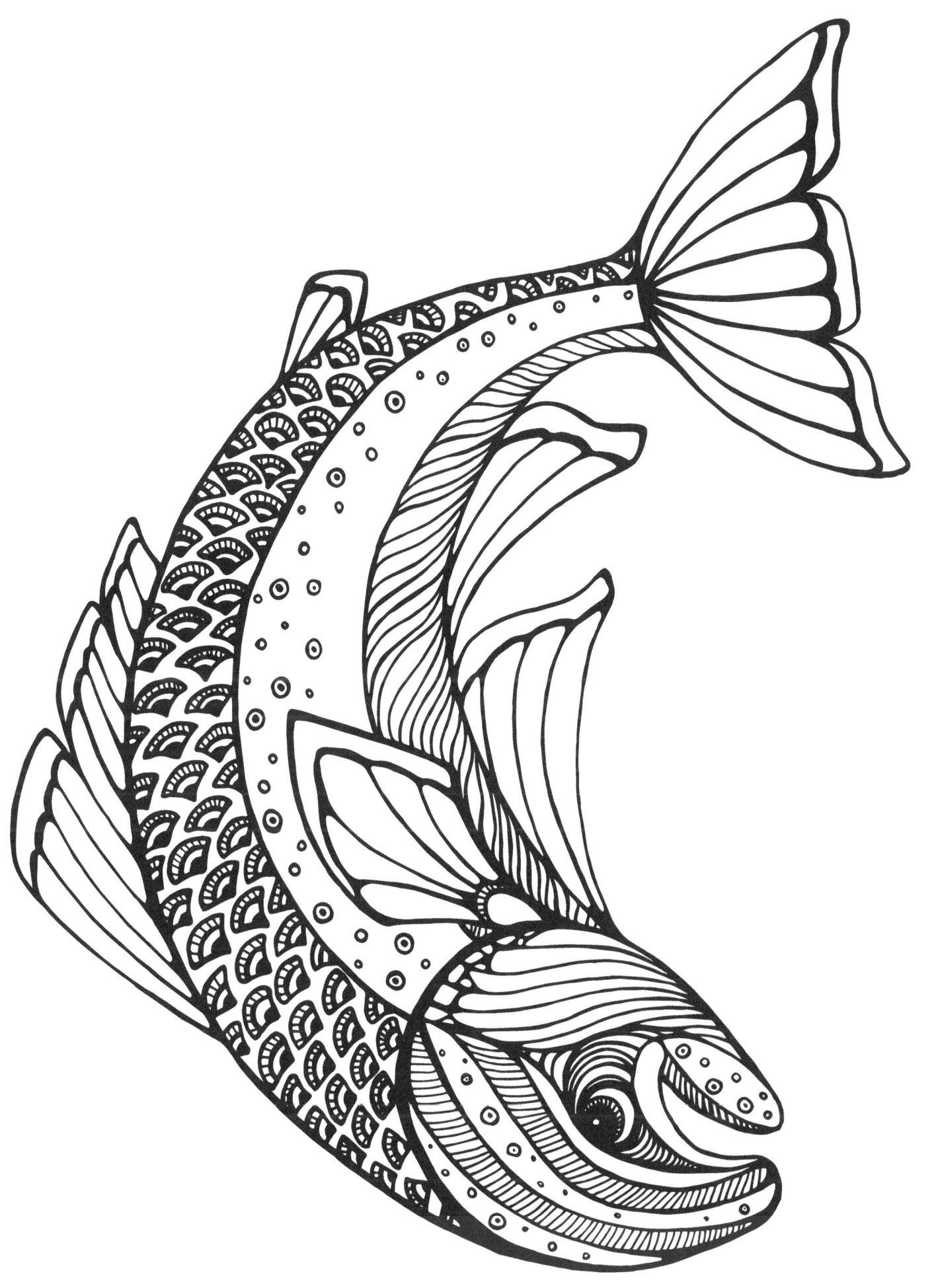

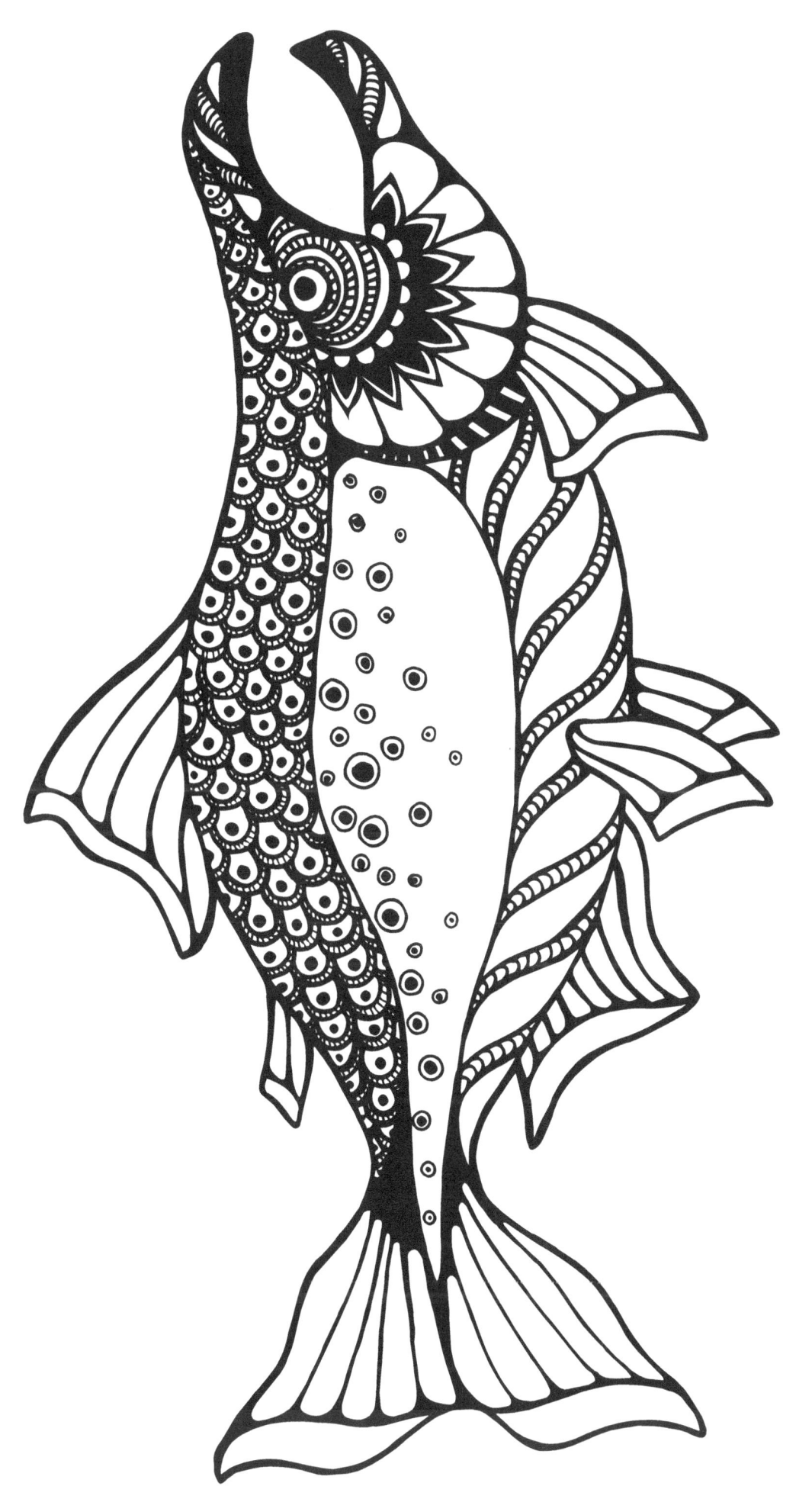

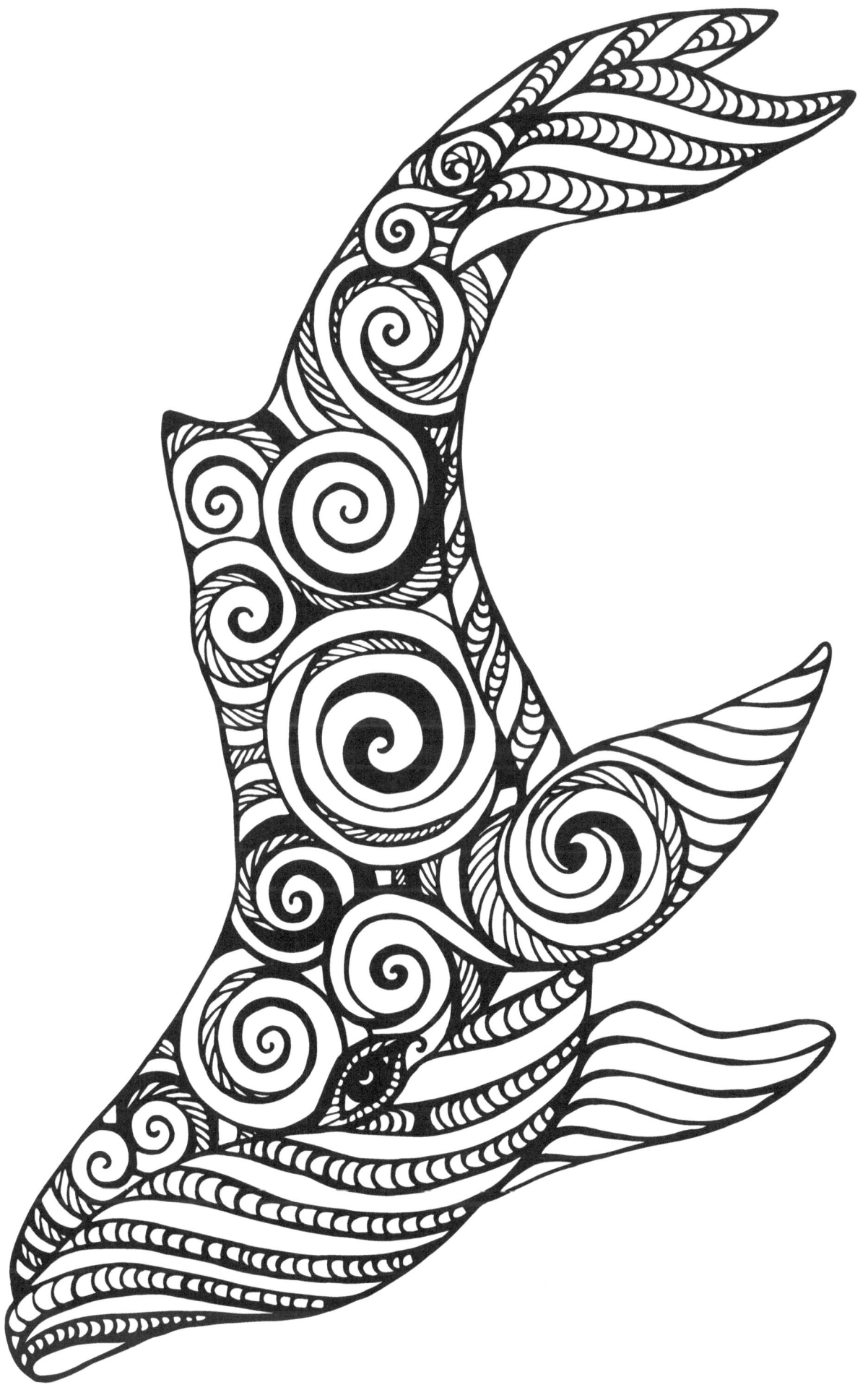

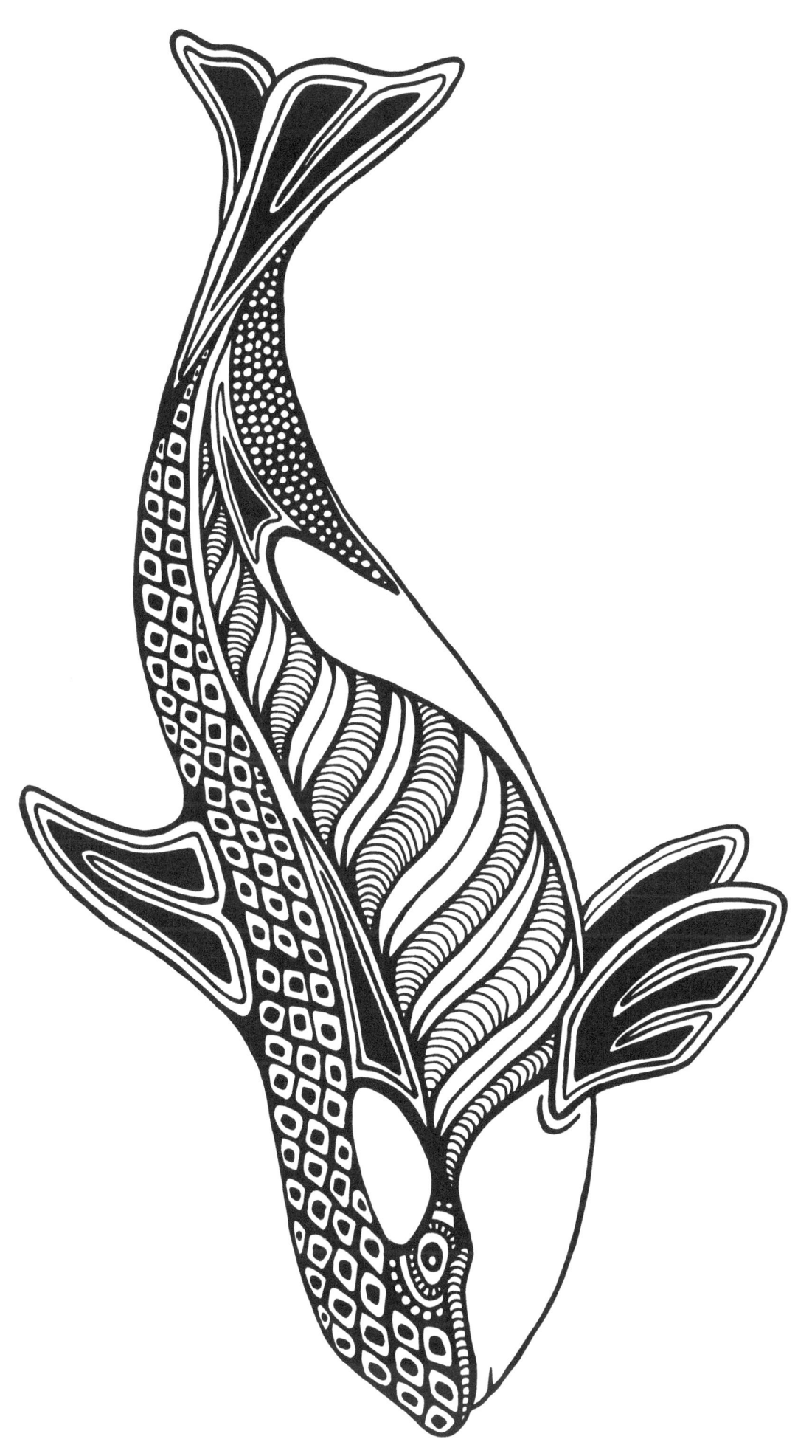

Feeling inspired? Draw your own design here

www.ingramcontent.com/pod-product-compliance
Lightning Source LLC
Chambersburg PA
CBHW080649180526
45168CB00008B/3357